# NEW DANGERS

# TO FREEDOM,

AND

# NEW DUTIES

# FOR ITS DEFENDERS:

A LETTER

BY THE

HON. HORACE MANN

TO HIS CONSTITUENTS,

MAY 3, 1850.

BOSTON:
REDDING AND COMPANY,
1850.

DAMRELL & MOORE, PRINTERS, NO. 16 DEVONSHIRE STREET.

# LETTER.

---

West Newton, May 3, 1850.

To the Honorable James Richardson, I. Cleveland, and John Gardner, of Dedham; Honorable D. A. Simmons, John J. Clarke, Francis Hilliard and George R. Russell, of Roxbury, &c.

Gentlemen: — Having been called home on account of sickness in my family, I have just received, at this place, your kind invitation to meet and address my constituents of the 8th Congressional District, and to give them my "*views and opinions upon the question of the immediate admission of California, and other questions now before Congress arising out of the acquisition of territory by the treaty with Mexico.*"

A request from so high a source has almost the force of a command. Yet I dare not promise to comply. I am liable at any moment to be recalled, and, instead of speaking here, to vote there, upon the questions to which you refer. I might be summoned to return on the day appointed for us to meet. The only alternative, therefore, which is left me, is to address you by letter. This I will do, if I can find time. I shall thus comply with your request, in substance, if not in form.

On many accounts, I have the extremest reluctance to appear before the public on the present occasion. My views, on some vital questions, differ most materially from those of gentlemen for whom I have felt the profoundest respect; and for some of whom I cherish the strongest personal attachment. But I feel, on the other hand, that my constituents, having entrusted to me some of their most precious interests, are entitled to know my "views and opinions" respecting the hopes and the dangers that encompass them. I shall not, therefore, take the responsibility of declining.

I will premise further, that my relations to political parties, for many years past, have left me as free from all partisan bias "as the lot of humanity will admit." For twelve years I held an office whose duties required me to abstain from all active coöperation in political conflicts; and that duty was so religiously fulfilled, that, to my knowledge, I was never charged with its violation. During the Presidential contest of 1848, those obligations of neutrality still rested upon me. For a year afterwards, I was not called upon to do any official act displeasing to any party amongst us. This interval I employed in forming the best opinion I could of public men and measures, and their influence upon the moral and industrial interests of the country. I had long entertained most decided convictions in favor of protecting American labor, in favor of cheap postage, and of security to the lives and property of our fellow-citizens engaged in commerce. But a new question had arisen,— the great question of Freedom or Slavery in our recently acquired territories,— and this question I deemed, for the time being, to be, though not exclusive of others, yet paramount to them. Or rather, I saw that nothing could be so favorable to all the last named interests, as the proper adjustment of the first. He who would provide for the welfare of mankind must first provide for their liberty.

Sympathizing, then, on different points with different parties, but exclusively bound to none, I stood, in reference to the great question of territorial freedom or slavery, in the position of the *true* mother in the litigation before Solomon, preferring that the object of my love should be spared in the hands of any one, rather than perish in my own.

Our present difficulties, which, as you well know, have arrested the gaze of the nation, and almost suspended the legislative functions of Congress, pertain to the destiny of freedom or of slavery, to which our new territories are to be consigned. After the acquisition of Louisiana, and Florida, and Texas, for the aggrandizement and security of the slave power; after the aboriginal occupants of the soil of the Southern States have been slaughtered, or driven from their homes, at an expense of not less than a hundred millions of dollars, and at the infinite expense of our national reputation for justice and humanity; and after the area of the Slave States has been made almost double that of the Free States, while the population of the Free is about double that of the Slave; the reasons seem so strong that they can hardly be made stronger, why the career of our government as a slavery-extending power, should be arrested. On the other hand, the oligarchy who rule the South, seeing that, notwithstanding their rich and almost illimitable domain, they are rapidly falling behind the North in all the distinctive elements of civilization and well-being,—industry, temperance, education, wealth,—not only defend the Upas that blasts their soil, as though it were the Tree of Life, but seek to transplant it to other lands. With but about three slaves to a square mile,—three millions of slaves to nearly a million of square miles,—they say they are too crowded, that they feel a sense of suffocation, and must have more room, when all their weakness and pain proceed, not from the limited quantity, but from the bad quality of the atmosphere they breathe. Hence the war with Mexico, commenced and prosecuted to add slave territory and slave States to the Southern section. Hence the refusal to accept propositions of peace, unless territory *south* of latitude 36 deg. 30 min. (the Missouri compromise line, so called), should be ceded to us. Hence when the Mexican negotiators proposed to insert a prohibition of slavery in the treaty of cession, and declared that the Inquisition would not be more odious to the American people than the reinstitution of slavery to them, our minister, Mr. Trist, told them he would not consent to such a prohibition, though they would cover the soil a foot deep with gold. And hence, also, the determination of a portion of the Southern members of Congress, to stop the whole machinery of government, to sacrifice all the great interests of the country, and assail even the Union itself, unless slavery shall be permitted to cross the Rio Grande, and enter the vast regions of the West, as it heretofore crossed the Mississippi and the Sabine.

Even in 1846, when the war against Mexico was declared, all men of sagacity foresaw the present conflict. Could that question have been decided on its merits; or could the institutions to be planted upon the territory we might acquire, be determined by the unbiased suffrages of the American people, no war would have been declared, and no territory acquired. But the great political leaders of the South expected to make up both for their numerical weakness and for the injustice of their cause, by connecting the question of slavery-extension with that of future Presidential elections, and with the strife of parties. They promised themselves that they could draw over leading Northern men to their support, by offering them the Tantalus cup of Presidential honors; and then by the force of party cohesion and discipline ensure the support of the whole descending-scale of office expectants. Early in the present session of Congress, it was distinctly declared from a high Southern source, that the South must do most for those Northern men who would do most for them. A few words will make it apparent how faithfully this plan has been adhered to, and how successful it is likely to become.

No Northern Democrat, opposed to slavery extension, could expect the support of the Southern Democracy. Hence, Gen. Cass stept promptly forward, and declared in his Nicholson letter, that Congress had no power to exclude slavery from the territories. This has been technically called his "bid," or his "first bid." It was deemed satisfactory by the South; for, according to their philosophy, the relation of master and slave is the natural or normal relation of mankind; and therefore, where no prohibition of it exists, slavery flows into free territory, as water runs down hill. This avowal of Gen. Cass was rendered more signal and valuable to the South, because, for the greater part of his political life, he had taken oaths, held offices and administered laws, in undeniable contradiction to the declaration then made. The Ordinance of 1787 was expressly recognized by the First Congress, held under the Constitution, [See ch. 8.] It was modified in part, and confirmed as to the rest; and in holding offices under this, Gen. Cass had laid the foundation of his honors and his fortune. His declaration, therefore, against all interdiction of slavery, made under circumstances so extraordinary and in contradiction of the whole tenor of his past life, was hailed with acclamation by the South, and he was unanimously declared, at Baltimore, to be the accepted candidate of the Democracy, for the office of President. The common notion is that a man shows his love for a cause by the amount of sacrifice he will make for it; and as consistency, honor and truth, are the most precious elements in character, who could sacrifice more than he!

To the honor of the Whig party be it said, there was not a Northern man to be found, who, to gain the support of the South, would espouse its pro-slavery doctrines, or invent any new reading of the Constitution to give them a semblance of law. Hence, at the Philadelphia Convention, no Northern Whig received even so much as a complimentary vote. The judicial eminence of Judge McLean, the military eminence of Gen. Scott, were passed contemptuously by; and Mr. Webster, acknowledged to be the greatest statesman of the age, received but fourteen votes, out of almost three hundred; and twelve of these were from Massachusetts. Mr. Webster had spoken more eloquent words for Liberty than any other living man, and this distinguished neglect was doubtless intended to teach him the lesson, that the path to Presidential honors did not lie through an advocacy of the rights of man. Gen. Taylor was nominated and chosen. He was understood to take neutral ground. Discountenancing the veto power, yet, if the House of Representatives, who are chosen directly from and by the people, and the Senate who are chosen by the States, will pass a territorial bill, either with or without a prohibition of slavery, he will approve it. This is the common opinion, and I have no doubt of its correctness.

Under these circumstances, a most desperate effort was made at the close of the last Congress to provide a government for the territories, with no prohibtion of slavery. Had Gen. Cass been elected, no such effort would have been necessary, for he was pledged to veto a prohibition. Gen. Taylor was supposed to be pledged to an opposite course; and hence the struggle. The facts must be so fresh in the recollection of all that they hardly need to be recounted. The House performed its duty to the country and to freedom, by sending territorial bills to the Senate, containing the prohibitory clause. The Senate, equalling the northern by its southern votes, and far out-numbering the Whigs by its Democrats, left those bills to sleep the sleep of death upon its table. But during the closing hours of the session, it foisted a provision for the government of the territories, into the general appropriation bill; and held out the menace that this bill should not pass at all, unless the territorial clause should pass with it. The flagitiousness of this proceeding, it is difficult to comprehend and impossible to describe. The appropriation bill is one on which the working, and even the continuance of the government depend. Without it the machinery of the State must cease to move. Contracts by the government to pay money must be violated. Officers cannot obtain their salaries. Families must be left without subsistence. If long continued, all judges would resign and courts be broken up; and when justice should cease to be administered, violence, robbery, and every form of crime would run riot through the land.

Besides, an appropriation bill and a bill for the government of territories, have no congruity with each other; they are not relevant; neither is germane to the other. Every one knows it to be a common parliamentary rule that when a proposition is submitted which is susceptible of division, any *one* member has a right to demand it. All bills, too, for raising revenue must, by the Constitution, originate in the House; and the House has as much right to interfere to prevent the Senate from ratifying a treaty, as the Senate has to obstruct the passage of a revenue bill, by adding to it extraneous provisions. It was this effort on the part of the Senate to incorporate into the appropriation bill a provision most unrighteous in itself and most odious to the free sentiments of the North, which led to the protracted session on the night of the 3d of March, 1849. The course of the pro-slavery leaders, on that occasion, resembled that of a madman who should seize a torch, and stand over the magazine of a ship, and proclaim that he would send men and vessel to destruction, unless they would steer for his port. A portion of the House confederated with the majority of the Senate, in this unprincipled machination; but the larger number stood undaunted, and after perils such as so precious an interest never before encountered, the pro-slavery amendment was stricken out, and its champions were foiled. Through that memorable night, the friends of freedom wrestled like Jacob with the angel of God, and though the session did not close until the sun of a Sabbath morning shone full into the windows of the Capitol, yet a holier work never was done on that holy day.

It was with a joy such as no words can ever express, that I saw the territories rescued from the clutch of slavery by the expiration of the Thirtieth Congress. I felt confident that when the Thirty-first Congress should assemble, it would be under better auspices, and with a stronger phalanx on the side of freedom. In regard to California, those hopes have been fulfilled; but I proceed to state how they have been nearly extinguished in regard to the residue of the territory.

Our first disaster was the election of a most adroit, talented and zealous pro-slavery Speaker. A better organ for the accomplishment of their purposes the friends of Slavery could not have found, nor the friends of Freedom a more formidable opponent. Whilst the pro-slavery champions of the South, almost without distinction of party, exulted over this triumph, it has been the occasion of most lamentable criminations and recriminations at the North. They abandon all distinctions of Whig or Democrat for the cause of Slavery; would to God we could do as much for the cause of Freedom.

The choice of a pro-slavery Speaker was immediately followed by the appointment of most ultra pro-slavery committees. Some Free Soil members, it is true, were placed upon these committees; but in this the Speaker only carried out more fully his own purposes and those of his party, by putting what they considered as insane men into close custody, instead of letting them run at large. He showed, however, either a want of courage in himself, or of confidence in his chosen guards; for, on the District of Columbia committee he detailed a file of five, on the Judiciary committee a file of four, and on the Territorial committee a file of six strong pro-slavery men for the safe keeping of one Free Soiler.

Within an hour after the House was organized, Mr. Root of Ohio submitted a resolution, instructing the Committee on Territories to report territorial bills, prohibiting slavery. Many true friends to freedom believed this movement to be ill-timed and unfortunate; and though the House then refused, by a handsome vote, to lay the resolution on the table, yet when it came up for consideration again, the first decision was reversed by about the same majority. There is abundant proof that the latter vote did not express the true sentiment of the House. Not a few voted against the resolution avowedly because of its paternity—thus spiting a noble son on account of its obnoxious father. Others repented of their votes as soon as they came to reflect that the record would go where their explanation could not accompany it.

But unfortunately, it was too late. There stands the record, to survive through all time, and to be read of all men. The champions of slavery seized upon this vote as a propitious omen. They derided and scouted the proviso with a fierceness unknown before. They shouted their threats of disunion with a more defiant tone, should any attempt at what they called its resurrection, be made. A speech was delivered, in which a massacre of a majority of the House was distinctly shadowed forth, so that not "a quorum should be left to do business." The effect of that vote was almost as bad as though it meant what it said.

At a later day, when a bill for the admission of California was presented, the tactics of delay were resorted to, and midnight found us calling the yeas and nays, for more than the thirtieth time, on questions whose frivolousness and vexatiousness cannot be indicated by numbers.

The proceedings in the Senate, however, are those which now threaten the most disastrous consequences. Early in the session, in order to bring his Northern friends up to the doctrine that it is unconstitutional to legislate upon slavery in the territories, Gen. Cass made a speech, in which he denies that Congress has *any* power, under *any* circumstances, to pass *any* law respecting their inhabitants. According to that speech, the United States stands in the relation of a foreign government to the people of its own territories; and if they set up a king or establish a religion, we cannot help it; for we have no more power or right to control them, than we have the subjects of Great Britain, or the citizens of France. It has been said that the doctrine of Gen. Cass and that of Gen. Taylor, on this subject, are identical; but there is this all-important difference between them: Gen. Taylor maintains the right of Congress to legislate for the territories, and will doubtless approve any bill for the prohibition of slavery in them; but Gen. Cass, denying this right in Congress, would, if President, veto such a bill. He, therefore, would leave the territories open to be invaded and possessed by slavery; and in Southern law and practice, possession is more than nine points.

Next came Mr. Clay's compromise resolutions, so called. By these, California was to be admitted as a State; the territories organized without any restriction upon slavery; the Southwestern boundary of Texas to be extended to the Rio Grande; a part of her twelve or fifteen million debt to be paid by the United States, on condition of her abandoning her claim to that part of New Mexico which lies east of the Rio Grande; the abolition of the slave trade in the District of Columbia, and the inviolability of slavery in the District during the good pleasure of Maryland and of the inhabitants of the District; more effectual provision for the restitution of fugitive slaves, and free traffic in slaves forever between the States, unless forbidden by themselves.

A compromise is a settlement of difficulties by mutual concessions. Let us examine the mutuality of the concessions which Mr. Clay's resolutions propose.

In the first place, California is to be permitted to remain free, if the territories of New Mexico and Utah may be opened to slavery. But California is free already; free by her own act; free without any concession of theirs, and without any grace but the grace of God. It is mainly occupied by a Northern population, who do their own work, with their own hands, or their own brains. Fifty hardy gold diggers from the North will never stand all day knee-deep in water, shovel earth, rock washers, &c., under a broiling sun, and see a man with his fifty slaves standing under the shade of a tree, or having an umbrella held over his head, with whip in hand, and without

wetting his dainty glove, or soiling his japanned boot, pocket as much at night as the whole of them together. Or rather, they will never suffer institutions to exist which tolerate such unrighteousness. California, therefore, is free; as free as Massachusetts; and Mr. Clay might as well have said in terms, that, whereas Massachusetts is free, therefore New Mexico and Utah shall be slave, or run the hazard of being so.

The next point of Mr. Clay's compromise is, that Texas shall extend her Southwestern boundary from or near the Nueces to the Rio Grande, and shall receive, probably, some six or eight millions of dollars for withdrawing her claim to that part of New Mexico which lies east of the last named river. Now, Texas has no rightful or plausible claim to a foot of all this territory. But suppose it to be a subject of doubt, and therefore of compromise. The mutuality, then, consists in dividing the whole territory claimed by Texas, and then giving her a valid title to one portion of it, and paying her for all the rest. Texas, or,—what in this connection is the same thing,—slavery, surrenders absolutely nothing, gets a good title to some hundred thousand square miles of territory, and pay for as much more!

But what renders it almost incredible that any man could soberly submit such a proposition and dare to call it a compromise, is this: All that part of New Mexico which Texas claims, and which lies between the parallels of 36° 30′ and 42°, is, by the Resolutions of Annexation, to be forever free. I shall consider the constitutionality of these resolutions by and by; I now treat them as valid. Now the compromise proposes to buy this territory, so secured to freedom, and annex it to New Mexico, which is to be left open to slavery. We are to peril all the broad region between 36° 30′ and 42°, and pay Texas some six or eight millions of dollars for the privilege of doing so! Mr. Clay is not less eminent for his statesmanship than for his waggery. Were he to succeed in playing off this practical joke upon the North, and were it not for the horrible consequences which it would involve, a roar of laughter, like a *feu de joie*, would run down the course of the ages. As it is, the laughter will be "Elsewhere."

The next point pertains to the abolition of the slave trade, and the perpetuity of slavery in the District of Columbia. This District has an area of about fifty square miles; and Mr. Clay proposes, in consideration of transferring its slave marts to Alexandria, on the Virginia side, or to some convenient place in Montgomery or Prince George's county, on the Maryland side, to divest Congress forever of its right of "exclusive legislation" over it. Should this plan prevail, the perpetuity of slavery in the District will be defended by more unassailable and impregnable barriers than any other institution in Christendom. The President has a veto upon Congress; but two-thirds of both houses may still pass any law, notwithstanding his dissent. Mr. Clay proposes to give, both to Maryland and to the citizens of the District, a veto on this subject; — an absolute veto, not a qualified one, like that of the President of the United States, but one that will control, not majorities merely, but an absolute unanimity in both branches of Congress. By his plan, therefore, three separate, independent powers are to have a veto upon the abolition of slavery in the District of Columbia. And not only so, but while it will require their *joint* or *concurrent* action to abolish the institution, any one of them can preserve it. The laws of the Medes and Persians had no such guaranties for perpetuity as this.

Mr. Clay's last point is really too facetious. So solemn a subject does not permit such long-continued levity, however it may be masked by sobriety of countenance. It is that Congress shall make more effectual provision for the capture and delivery of fugitive slaves; and, as an equivalent for this, it shall bind itself never to interfere with the inter-State traffic in slaves. We are to catch their slaves, and, as though that were a grateful privilege to us, we are to allow them free commerce in slaves, coastwise or inland. By this means, slaves can be transported to the mouth of the Rio Grande, and some hundreds of miles up that river, towards New Mexico, instead of being driven in coffles across the country. The compromise is, that for every slave we catch, we are to facilitate the passage of a hundred into New Mexico.

Such is the mutuality of Mr. Clay's compromises. They are such compromises as the wolf offers to the lamb, or the vulture to the dove. They make the rightful admission of California into the Union, with her free constitution, contingent upon opening the new territories to slavery; they ratify one part of the predatory claim of Texas, and propose to give her millions for the other part; they give an unconditional veto to the State of Maryland and to the citizens of the District of Columbia, over a unanimous vote of both Houses of Congress, even when approved by the President; in connection with Mr. Butler's bill and Mr. Mason's amendments, they expose our white citizens to grievous penalties and imprisonments for not doing what the Supreme Court of the United States has decided we are not bound to do, in relation to fugitive slaves, and they offer our colored citizens to be kidnapped and spirited away into bondage; and they foreclose, in favor of the South, the disputed question of the inter-State commerce in slaves. In one particular only do they appear to concede anything to Northern rights, or Northern convictions, or Northern feelings. They propose to transfer the District of Columbia slave-trade across an ideal line into Virginia or into Maryland, so that the slave-planter or slave-trader, when he comes to our American Congo to replenish his stock of human cattle, shall be obliged to go a mile or two, to the slave-marts, instead of walking down Pennsylvania Avenue. I deem this to be no concession. If it is honorable to produce corn and cotton, it is honorable to buy and sell them; and, if it is honorable to hold beings created in God's image, in slavery, it is honorable to stand between the producer and the consumer, and to make merchandise of the bodies and the souls of men. Let this Light of the Age be set upon a hill that all nations may behold it.

I will refer to Mr. Bell's resolutions no further than to say that they propose the formation of three slaves States out of what is now claimed by Texas, one of which is to be admitted into the Union forthwith as an offset to California.

Mr. Buchanan has not regarded the movements of his rival, Gen. Cass, with indifference. He has spent a considerable portion of the winter in Washington, and it is understood that he holds out the Missouri compromise line, from the Western boundary of Missouri to the Pacific Ocean, as his lune to the South, for their favorable regards in the ensuing Presidential contest.

In a chronological order I must now consider some vitally important views, which have been submitted by some members in the House, and by Mr. Webster and others in the Senate. In mentioning the name of this great statesman, and in avowing that I am one among the many whom his recently expressed opinions have failed to convince, it is due to myself, however indifferent it may be to him or to his friends, that I should express my admiration of his powers, my gratitude for his past services, and the diffidence with which I dissented, at first, from his views. But I have pondered upon them long, and the longer I have pondered, the more questionable they appear. I shall therefore venture upon the perilous task of inquiring into their correctness; and while I do it with the deference and respect which belong to his character, I shall do it also with that fidelity to conscience and to judgment that belong to mine. He is great, but truth is greater than us all.

I shall confine myself mainly, and perhaps wholly, to Mr. Webster's views, because he has argued the cause of the South with vastly more ability than it has been argued by any one among themselves. If his conclusions, then, be not tenable, their case is lost.*

Mr. Webster casts away the "Proviso" altogether. He says "*if a resolution or a law were now before us to provide a territorial government for New Mexico, I would not vote to put any prohibition into it whatever;*" p. 44. The reason given is, that slavery is already excluded from "California and New Mexico" "by the law of nature, of physical geography, the law of the formation of the earth." p. 42. "California and New Mexico are Asiatic in their formation and scenery. They are composed of vast

*All my quotations from Mr. Webster are taken from the edition of his speech which he dedicated to the "PEOPLE OF MASSACHUSETTS," March 18, 1850. Among the numerous readings which have appeared, I suppose this to be the most authentic.

ridges of mountains of enormous height, with broken ridges and deep valleys;" p. 43.

Now this is drawing moral conclusions from physical premises. It is arguing from physics to metaphysics. It is determining the law of the spirit by geographical phenomena. It is undertaking to settle by mountains and rivers, and not by the Ten Commandments, a great question of human duty. It abandons the second commandment of Christ and all Bills of Rights enacted in conformity thereto, and leaves our obligations to our "neighbor" to be determined by the accidents of earth and water and air. To ascertain whether a people will obey the divine command, and do to others as they would be done by, it looks at the thermometer. What a problem would this be? "Required the height above the level of the sea, at which the oppressor 'will undo the heavy burdens and let the oppressed go free, and break every yoke,'—to be determined barometrically." Alas! this cannot be done. Slavery depends, not upon Climate, but upon Conscience. Wherever the wicked passions of the human heart can go, there slavery can go. Slavery is an effect. Avarice, sloth, pride, and the love of domination are its cause. In ascending mountain sides, at what altitude do men leave these passions behind them? Different vegetable growths are to be found at different heights, depending also upon the zone. This I can understand. There is the altitude of the palm, the altitude of the oak, the altitude of the pine, and far above them all the line of perpetual snow. But in regard to innocence and guilt, where is the *white line?* How high up can a slave-holder go and not lose his free agency? At what elevation will the whip fall from the hand of the master, and the fetter from the limbs of the slave? There is no such point. Freedom and slavery on the one hand, and climate and geology on the other, are incommensurable quantities. We might as well attempt to determine a question in theology by the cube root, or a question in ethics by the Black Art. Slavery being a crime founded upon human passions can go wherever those passions are unrestrained. It has existed in Asia from the earliest ages, notwithstanding its "formation and scenery." It labors and groans on the flanks of the Ural mountains now. There are to-day forty-eight millions of slaves in Russia, not one rood of which comes down so low as the Northern boundary of California and New Mexico.

Had Mr. Webster's philosophy been correct, then California was at superfluous pains when she incorporated the Ordinance of 1787 into her Constitution. Instead of saying that "slavery and involuntary servitude, (except for crime,) shall be forever prohibited," she should have said "Whereas by a law of nature, of physical geography, the law of the formation of the earth,"—"slavery cannot exist in California," therefore we will not "reaffirm an ordinance and statute, nor reënact the will of God."

Should it be said that slavery will not go into the new territories, because it is unprofitable, I ask where is it profitable? Where is ignorance so profitable as knowledge? Where is ungodliness gain, even for the things of this life? How little is the hand worth at one end of an arm, if there is not a brain at the other? Do not Maryland, Virginia, North Carolina, and other States, furnish witnesses by thousands and tens of thousands, that slavery impoverishes? Yet with what enthusiasm they cherish it. Generally, ignorance is a necessary concomitant of slavery. Of white persons, over twenty years of age, unable to read and write, there were, according to the last census, 58,787 in Virginia, 56,609 in North Carolina, 58,513 in Tennessee, and so forth. I have a letter before me received this morning, dated in Indiana, in which the writer says he removed from North Carolina, in 1802, when he was fourteen years old, and at that time he had never seen a newspaper in his life. Can there be genius, the inventive talent, or profitable labor, where ignorance is so dense? Can the oppression that tramples out voluntary industry, intelligence, enterprise, and the desire of independence, conduce to riches? Yet this is done wherever slavery exists, and is part and parcel of its working. Is any other form of robbery profitable? Yet individuals and communities have practised it and lived by it, and we may as well rely upon a "law of physical geography" to arrest the one as the other. It is not poetry, but literal truth, that the breath of the slave blasts vegetation, his tears poison the earth, and his groans strike it with sterility. It would be easy to show why the master does not abandon slavery, even amid the desolation with which it has surrounded him. There is a combination of poverty and pride, which slavery produces, *on the doctrine of natural appetence*, and which, therefore, it exactly fits. The helplessness of the master in regard to all personal wants, seems to necessitate the slavery that has begotten it. All moral and religious principles are lowered till they conform to the daily practice. Custom blinds conscience, until, without any attempt to emancipate or ameliorate their victims, men can preach and pray and hold slaves, as Hamlet's grave-digger jests and sings while he turns up skulls.

But slavery cannot go into California or New Mexico, because their staple productions are not "tobacco, corn, cotton or rice;" p. 44. These are agricultural products. But is slave labor confined to agriculture? Suppose that predial slavery will not become common in the new territories. Cannot menial? If slaves cannot do field-work, cannot they do house-work? There is an opening for a hundred thousand slaves to-day, and in the new territories, for purposes of domestic labor. And beyond this, let me ask, who posesses any such geologic vision that, at the distance of a thousand miles, he can penetrate the valleys and gorges of New Mexico, and say that gold will not yet be found there as it is in California,—not in sand and gravel only, but in forty-eight pounders and in fifty-sixes? This is the very kind of labor on which slaves, in all time, have been so extensively employed,—the very labor on which a million of slaves in Hispaniola lost their lives, within a few years after its discovery by Columbus. Gold deposits are now worked within twenty-five miles of Santa Fe. The last account which I have seen, of a company of emigrants passing from Santa Fe to California by the river Gila, announces rich discoveries of gold upon that river. A fellow-citizen of mine has just returned home, who says he saw a slave sold at the mines in California, in September last. As yet, the distant regions of the Gila and the Colorado cannot be worked, because of the Apaches, the Utahs, and other tribes of Indians. But admit slavery there, and the power of the government will be invoked to exterminate these Indians, as it was before to exterminate the Cherokees and Seminoles,—not to drive them beyond the Mississippi, but beyond the Styx. A few days since a letter was published in the papers, dated on boaad a steamer descending the Mississippi, which stated that a considerable number of slaves were on board, bound for California, uuder an agreement with their masters that they should be free after serving two years at the mines. We know, too, that the rèason assigned for incorporating a provision in the constitution of California, authorizing its Legislature to pass laws for the exclusion of free blacks from the State, was that slaves would be brought there under this very form of agreement, and, by and by, the country would be overspread by people of color who had bought their freedom. The sagacious men who framed the California constitution came from all parts of the territory, and, being collected on the spot, having surveyed all its mountains, having breathed its air at all temperatures, and turned up its golden soil,—these men had never discovered any "law of physical geography" which the fell spirit of slavery could not transgress. Slaves were carried into Oregon, ten degrees of latitude higher up. Its colonists reënacted the Ordinance of 1787, before Congress gave them a territorial government. In the territorial government that was given them, the prohibition was inserted; and President Polk signed the bill, with an express protest, that he ratified this exclusion of slavery only because the country lay north of the Missouri compromise line; but declared that, had it embraced the very region in question, he would have vetoed the bill.

Gen. Cass never took the ground that slavery could not exist in the new territories; and no inconsiderable part of the opposition made to him in Massachusetts and in other free States, was placed expressly upon the ground that he would not prohibit it. Mr. Webster, in his Marshfield speech, Sept. 1, 1848, opposed the election of Gen. Cass, because, through his recreancy to Northern principles, slavery would invade the territories. This was expressed with his usual clearness and force, as follows:

"He, [Gen. Cass,] will surely have the Senate; and with the patronage of the government, with every interest that he, as a Northern man, can bring to bear, coöperaring with every interest that the South can bring to bear, we cry safety before we are out of the woods, *if we feel that there is no danger as to these new territories.*"

Yet Mr. Webster now says that to support the "Proviso," would "do disgrace to his own understanding;" p. 46.

During the same campaign, also, the Honorable Rufus Choate, one of the most eloquent men in New England, and known to be the personal friend of Mr. Webster, delivered a speech at Salem, in which the following passage occurs:

"It is the passage of a law to say that California and New Mexico shall remain forever free. That is, fellow-citizens, undoubtedly, an object of great and transcendent importance; for there is none who will deny that we should go up to the very limits of the Constitution itself, and with the wisdom of the wisest, and zeal of the most zealous, should unite to accomplish this great object, and to defeat the always detested, and forever to be detested object of the dark ambition of that candidate of the Baltimore Convention, who has ventured to pledge himself in advance that he will veto the future law of freedom; and may God avert the madness of all those who hate slavery and love freedom, that would unite in putting him in the place where his thrice accursed pledge may be redeemed! . . . . Is there a Whig upon this floor who doubts that the strength of the Whig party next March will ensure freedom to California and New Mexico, if by the Constitution they are entitled to freedom at all? Is there a member of Congress that would not vote for freedom? You know there is not one. Did not every Whig member of Congress from the free States vote at the last session for freedom? You know that every man of them returned home covered with the thanks of his constituents for that vote. Is there a single Whig constituency, in any free State in this country, that would return any man that would not vote for freedom? *Do you believe that Daniel Webster himself could be returned if there was the least doubt upon the question?*"

Mr. Choate then adds: — "Upon this question alone, we always differ from those Whigs of the South; and on that one, we *propose simply to vote them down.*" Mr. Webster now says he will not join in voting them down.

Under such circumstances is it frivolous or captious to ask for something more than a dogmatic assertion that slavery cannot impregnate these new regions, and cause them to breed monsters forever? On a subject of such infinite importance I cannot be satisfied with a dictum; I want a demonstration. I cannot accept the prophecy without inquiring what spirit inspired the prophet. As a revelation from heaven it would be most delightful; but, as it conflicts with all human experience, it requires at least one undoubted miracle to attest the divinity of its origin.

According to the last census, there were more than eight thousand persons of African blood in Massachusetts. Abolish the moral and religious convictions of our people, let slavery appear to be in their sight not only lawful and creditable, but desirable as a badge of aristocratic distinction, and as a "political, social, moral and religious blessing," and what obstacle would prevent these eight thousand persons from being turned into slaves, on any day, by the easy, cheap and short-hand kidnapping of a legislative act? Africans can exist here, for the best of all reasons,—they do exist here. A state of slavery would not stop their respiration, nor cause them to vanish "into thin air." Think, for a moment, of the complaints we constantly hear in certain circles, of the difficulty and vexatiousness of commanding domestic service. If no moral or religious objection existed against holding slaves, would not many of those respectable and opulent gentlemen who signed the letter of thanks to Mr. Webster, and hundreds of others indeed, instead of applying to intelligence offices, or visiting emigrant ships for domestics, as we call them, go at once to the auction-room and buy a man or a woman with as little hesitancy or compunction as they now send to Brighton for beeves, or go to Tattersall's for a horse? If the cold of the higher latitudes checks the flow of African blood, or benumbs African limbs, the slaveholder knows very well that a trifling extra expense for whips will make up for the difference.

But suppose a doubt could be reasonably entertained about the invasion of the new territories by slavery. Even suppose the chances to preponderate against it. What then? Are we to submit a question of human liberty, over vast regions and for an indefinite extent of time, to the determination of chance? With all my faculties I say *No!* Let me ask any man, let me respectfully ask Mr. Webster himself, if it were his own father and mother, and brothers and sisters, and sons and daughters, who were in peril of such a fate, whether he would abandon them to chance,—even to a favorable chance. Would he suffer their fate to be determined by dice or divination, when positive prohibition was in his power? And by what rule of Christian morality, or even of enlightened heathen morality, can we deal differently with the kindred of others from what we would with our own? He is not a Christian whose humanity is bounded by the legal degrees of blood, or by general types of feature.

But Mr. Webster would not "taunt" the South. Neither would I. I would not taunt any honorable man, much less a criminal. Still, when the most precious interests of humanity are in peril, I would not be timid. I would not stop too long to cull lovers' phrases. Standing under the eye of God, in the forum of the world and before the august tribunal of posterity, when the litigants are Freedom and Tyranny, and human happiness and human misery the prize they contest, it should happen to the sworn advocate

2

of Liberty, as Quintilian says it did to Isocrates, "not to speak and to plead, but to thunder and to lighten." Mr. Webster would not taunt the South; and yet I say the South were never so insulted before, as he has insulted them. Common scoffs, jeers, vilifications, are flattery and sycophancy, compared with the indignities he heaped upon them. Look at the facts. The South waged war with Mexico from one and only one motive; for one and only one object,—the extension of slavery. They refused peace unless it surrendered territory. That territory must be south of the abhorred line of 36 deg. 30 min. The same President who abandoned the broad belt of country on our northern frontier, from 49 deg. to 54 deg. 40 min., to which we had, in his own words, "an unquestionable title," would allow no prohibition of slavery to be imposed upon the territory which Mexico ceded, though she would bury it a foot deep in gold. The Proviso had been resisted in all forms, from the beginning. Southern Whigs voted against the ratification of the treaty, foreseeing the struggle that was to follow. Desperate efforts were made to smuggle in an unrestricted territorial government, against all parliamentary rule and all constitutional implication. The whole South, as one man, claimed it as a "describable, weighable, estimable, tangible" and most valuable "right," to carry slaves there. Calhoun, Berrien, Badger, Mason, Davis,—the whole Southern phalanx, Whig and Democrat, pleaded for it, argued for it, and most of them declared themselves ready to fight for it; and yet Mr. Webster rises in his place, and tells them they are all moon-struck, hallucinated, fatuous; because "an ordinance of Nature and the will of God" had settled this question from the beginning of the world. Mr. Calhoun said, immediately after this speech, Give us free scope and time enough, and we will take care of the rest.

Mr. Mason said—

"We have heard here from various quarters and from high quarters, and repeated on all hands,—repeated here again to-day by the honorable Senator from Illinois, (Mr. Shields,) that there is a law of nature which excludes the Southern people from every portion of the State of California. I know of no such law of nature,—none whatever; but I do know the contrary, that if California had been organized with a territorial form of government only, and for which, at the last two sessions of Congress, she has obtained the entire Southern vote, the people of the Southern States would have gone there freely, and have taken their slaves there in great numbers. They would have done so because the value of the labor of that class would have been augmented to them many hundred fold. Why, in the debates which took place in the convention in California which formed the constitution, and which any Senator can now read for himself, after the provision excluding slavery was agreed upon, it was proposed to prohibit the African race altogether, free as well as bond. A debate arose upon it; and the ground was distinctly taken, as shown in those debates, that if the entire African race was not excluded, their labor would be found so valuable that the owners of slaves would bring them there, even though slavery were prohibited, under a contract to manumit them in two or three years. And it required very little reasoning, on the part of those opposed to this class of population, to show that the productiveness of their labor would be such as to cause that result. An estimate was gone into with reference to the value of the labor of this class of people, showing that it would be increased to such an extent in the mines of California, that they could not be kept out. It was agreed that the labor of a slave in any one of the States from which they would be taken, was not worth more than one hundred or one hundred and fifty dollars a year, and that in California it would be worth from four to six thousand dollars. They would work themselves free in one or two years, and thus the country would be filled by a class of free blacks, and their former owners have an excellent bargain in taking them there."

Yet Mr. Webster stands up before all this array, and says: "Gentlemen, you are beside yourselves. You have eaten hellebore. You would look more in character should you put on the 'cap and bells.' In sober sense, in seeing his object clearly and in pursuing it directly, Don Quixote was Dr. Franklin, compared with *you*. The dog in the fable, who dropped his meat to snap at its shadow, is no allegory in your case. I see two classes around me,—wise men and fools; *you* do not belong to the former. The Chancellor who keeps the king's idiots should have custody of you." Such is a faithful abstract of what Mr. Webster said to Southern Senators, and through them to all the South.

Here certainly was a reflection upon the understanding and intelligence of the South, such as never was cast upon them before. But the balm went with the sting. They bore the affront to their judgments, because it was so grateful to their politics and pockets. I think it no injustice to those Senators to say, that they would have nearly torn Mr. Webster in pieces for such a collective insult, if it had not promised to add fifty per cent. to their individual property, and to secure and perpetuate their political ascendancy.

To help our conceptions in regard to Mr. Webster's course on this subject, let us imagine a parallel case,—or rather, an approximate one, for there can be no parallel. Suppose a contest between the North and the South, on the subject of the Tariff, to have been raging for years. The sober blood of the North is heated to the fever-point. The newspapers treat of nothing else. Public meetings and private conversation discuss no other theme. Hundreds of delegates wait upon Congress, to add, if it be but a feather's weight, to the scale which holds their interests. Petitions flow in, in thousands and tens of thousands. It is announced that Mr. Calhoun will pour out his great mind on the subject. Expectation is on tiptoe. All eyes, from all sides of the country, are turned towards Washington, as the Muezzin's to Mecca. The Senate chamber is packed, and the illustrious Senator rises. After an historic sketch of existing difficulties; after reading from the speeches which he made in 1832, and in 1846, he proceeds to say that he withdraws all opposition to a tariff,—to any tariff! He will not offend the delicate nerves of Northern manufacturers by further hostility. Were a bill then before him, he would not oppose it. "Take the schedules," says he, scornfully, to Northern Senators, "and fill up the blanks from A to Z with what per-centages you please. For *ad valorem* rates, put in minimums and maximums at your pleasure. I will 'taunt' you no longer. I am for peace and the glorious Union. I have discovered an irrepealable and irreversible law of nature, which overrules all the devices of men. You cannot make one yard of woollens or cottons in New England. There, water has no gravity, steam has no force, and wheels will not revolve. In Vermont and New York, wool will not grow on sheeps' backs. I have penetrated the geology of Pennsylvania, and through all its stratifications, there is not a thimble-full of coal, nor an ounce of iron ore; and, if there were, combustion would not help to forge it; for oxygen and carbon are divorced. As Massachusetts contributed one-third of the men and one-third of the money, to carry on the Revolutionary War, I am willing to compensate her for her lost blood and treasure, to the amount of hundreds of millions of dollars, with which she may fertilize the barrenness of her genius, and indulge her insane love for churches and schools." Had the great Southern Senator spoken thus, I think that even idolatrous, man-worshipping South Carolina, —a State which Mr. Calhoun has ruled and moved for the last twenty-five years, as a puppet-showman plays Punch and Judy,—would have sent forth, through all her organs, a voice of unanimous dissent.

As much as Freedom is higher than Tariff, so much stronger than their dissent should be ours.

Mr. Webster's averment that he would not "re-affirm an ordinance of Nature, nor reënact the will of God," [p. 44,] has been commented on more pungently than I am able or willing to do. It has been said that all law and all volition must be in harmony with the will of the Good Spirit or with that of the Evil One; and, if we will not reënact the will of the former, then, either all legislation ceases, or we must register the decrees of the latter. But one important and pertinent consideration belongs to this subject, which I have nowhere seen developed. It is this: Endless doubts and contradictions exist among men, as to what is the will of God; and on no subject is there a wider diversity of opinion than on this very subject of slavery. Whose law was reënacted by the Ordinance of 1787? whose, when the African slave-trade was prohibited? whose, when it was declared piracy? True, it is useless to put upon our statute-books an astronomical law, regulating sunrise, or high tides; but that is physical and beyond the jurisdiction of man, while slavery belongs to morals, and is within the jurisdiction of man. Cease to transcribe upon the statute-book what our wisest and best men believe to be the will of God in regard to our worldly affairs, and the passions which we think appropriate to devils will soon take possession of society. In regard to slavery, piracy, and so forth, there are multitudes of men, whose fear of the penal sanctions of another life is very much aided by a little salutary fine and imprisonment in this. Look at that noble array of principles which is contained in the Declaration of Rights in the Constitution of Massachusetts. Is it not a most grand and beautiful exposition of "the will of God,"—a transcript as it were, from the Book of Life. So of the amendments to the Constitution of the United States. Yet our fathers thought it no tampering with holy things to enact them; and, in times of struggle and peril, they have been to many a tempted man as an anchor to the soul, sure and steadfast.

I approach Mr. Webster's treatment of the Texas question with no ordinary anxiety. Having been accustomed from my very boyhood to regard him as the almost infallible expounder of constitutional law, it is impossible to describe the struggle, the revulsion of mind, with which I have passed from an instructed and joyous acquiescence in his former opinions to unhesitating dissent from his present ones.

I must premise that I cannot see any necessary or beneficial connection between the subject of new Texan States and the admission of California and the government of the territories. The former refers to some indefinite future, when, from its fruitful womb of slavery, Texas shall seek to cast forth an untimely birth. In this excited state of the country,—at this critical juncture of our affairs, when there is sober talk of massacring a majority of the House of Representatives on their own floor, and a Senator, instead of threatening to hang a brother Senator on the highest tree, provided he could catch him in his own State, now draws a revolver of six barrels on another brother Senator, on the floor of the Senate, in mid session;—at such a time, I say, when, however few Abels there may be at work in the political field, there are Cains more than enough, would it not have been well to have said, "Sufficient unto the day is the evil thereof"?

As the basis of his argument, Mr. Webster quotes the following resolution:

> "New States of convenient size, not exceeding four in number, in addition to said State of Texas, and having sufficient population, may hereafter by the consent of the said State, be formed out of the territory thereof, which shall be entitled to admission under the provisions of the Federal constitution. And such States as may be formed out of that portion of said territory lying south of 36 deg. 30 min. north latitude, commonly known as the Missouri compromise line, shall be admitted into the Union, with or without slavery, as the people of each State asking admission may desire; and in such State or States as shall be formed out of said territory north of said Missouri compromise line, slavery or involuntary servitude, (except for crime,) shall be prohibited."

Note here, first, that only "*four*' States are to be admitted in "addition to said State of Texas;" and second, that "such State or *States*" (in the plural) as shall be formed from territory north of 36 deg., 30 min., *shall be free.* If *two*, or only *one* free State is to exist on the *north* side of the line, then how many will be left for the *south* side? I should expose myself to ridicule were I to set it down arithmetically, *four* minus *one*, equal to *three.* Yet Mr. Webster says "the guaranty is, that new States shall be made out of it, [the Texan territory,] and that such States as are formed out of that portion of Texas lying South of 36 deg., 30 min., may come in as slave States, to *the number of* FOUR, in addition to the State then in existence, and admitted at that time by these resolutions;" p. 29.

Here Mr. Webster gives outright to the South and to slavery, one more State than was contracted for,—assuming the contract to be valid. He makes a donation, a gratuity, of an entire slave State, larger than many a European principality. He transfers a whole State, with all its beating hearts, present and future, with all its infinite susceptibilities of weal or woe, from the side of freedom to that of slavery, in the leger-book of humanity. What a bridal gift for the harlot of bondage!

Was not the bargain hard enough, according to its terms? Must we fulfil it, and go beyond it? Is a slave State, which dooms our brethren of the human race, perhaps interminably, to the vassal's fate, so insignificant a trifle, that it may be flung in, as small change on the settlement of an account? Has the South been so generous a copartner, as to deserve this distinguished token of our gratitude?

Why, by parity of reasoning, could he not have claimed all the four States, "in addition to said State of Texas," as free States? The resolutions divide the territory into two parts, one north and one south of the line of 36° 30′. Could not Mr Webster have claimed the four States for Freedom with as sound logic, and with far better humanity than he surrendered them to Slavery? When Texas and the South have got their slave States "*to the number of four*" into the Union, whence are we to obtain our one or more free States? The contract will have been executed, and the consent of Texas for another State will be withheld.

Notwithstanding all this, Mr. Webster affirms the right of slavery to four more States, in the following words: "I know no form of legislation which can strengthen this. I know no mode of recognition that can add a tittle of weight to it." Catching the tone of his asseveration, I respond that I know no form of statement, nor process of reasoning, which can make it more clear that this is an absolute and wanton surrender of the rights of the North and the rights of humanity.

But I hold the Texan resolutions to have been utterly void; and proceed to give the reasons for my opinion.

I begin by quoting Mr. Webster against himself. In an Address to the people of the United States, from the Massachusetts Anti-Texas State Convention, January 29th, 1845, the subjoined passage, which is understood, or rather, I may say, is now well known, to have been dictated by Mr. Webster himself, may be found:

"But we desire not to be misunderstood. According to our convictions, there is no power in any branch of the government, or all its branches, to annex foreign territory to this Union. We have made the foregoing remarks only to show, that, if any fair construction could show such a power to exist any where, or to be exercised in any form, yet the manner of its exercise now proposed is *destitute of all decent semblance of constitutional propriety.*"

Thus cancelling the authority of Mr. Webster in 1850 by the authority of Mr. Webster in 1845, I proceed with the argument.

Though the annexation of Texas was in pursuance of a void stipulation, yet it is a clear principle of law that when a contract void between the parties, has been *executed* by them, it cannot then be annulled. If executed, it becomes valid, not by virtue of the contract, but by virtue of the execution. I bow to this legal principle, and would fulfil it. But any independent stipulation which remains unexecuted, remains invalid. Such is that part of the annexation resolutions which provides for the admission of a brood of Texan States. The resolutions themselves say in express terms, that the new States are to be admitted "under the provisions of the Federal Constitution;" and the Constitution says, "New States may be admitted *by the Congress* into this Union." By what Congress? Plainly, by the Congress in session at the time when application for admission is made; and by no other. The fourth Texan State may not be ready for admission for fifty years to come; and could the Congress of 1845 bind the Congress of 1900? The Congress of 1900 and all future Congresses, will derive their authority from the Constitution of the United States, and not from any preceding Congress. Put the case in a negative form. Could the Congress of 1845 bind all future Congresses *not* to admit new States, and thus, *pro tanto,* annul the Constitution? Positive or negative, the result is the same. No previous Congress, on such a subject, can enlarge or limit the power of a subsequent one. Whenever, therefore, the question of a new Texan State comes up for consideration, the Congress *then in being* must decide it on its own merits, untrammeled by anything their predecessors have done; and especially free from a law which, while similar in spirit, is a thousand times more odious in principle than statutes of mortmain.

Admitting that a future Congress, on such a subject, might be bound by a *treaty,* I answer that here was no treaty; while the fact that a treaty clause was introduced into the resolutions, in the Senate, for the sake of obtaining certain votes that would never otherwise have been given in their favor, and under an express pledge from the Executive that the method by treaty should be adopted, which pledge was forthwith iniquitously broken, leaves no element of baseness and fraud by wh h this proceeding was not contaminated. In the name of the Constitution, then, and of justice, let every honest man denounce those resolutions as void, alike in the forum of law and in the forum of conscience; and, admitting Texas herself to be in the Union, yet, when application is made for any new State from that territory, let the question be decided upon the merits it may then possess.

And was not Mr. Webster of the same opinion, when, in Faneuil Hall, in November, 1845, after the Resolutions of Annexation had passed, he made the following emphatic, but unprophetic, declaration :

"It is thought, it is an idea I do not say how well founded, that there may yet be a hope for resistance to the consummation of the act of annexation. I can only say for one that *if it should fall to my lot to have a vote on such a question*, AND I VOTE FOR THE ADMISSION INTO THIS UNION OF ANY STATE WITH A CONSTITUTION WHICH PROHIBITS EVEN THE LEGISLATURE FROM EVER SETTING THE BONDMEN FREE, I SHALL NEVER SHOW MY HEAD AGAIN, DEPEND UPON IT, IN FANEUIL HALL."

There is another objection to any future claim of Texas to be divided into States, which grows out of her own neglect to fulfil the terms and spirit of the agreement. In the "territory north of the Missouri compromise line, slavery or involuntary servitude, (except for crime,) shall be prohibited." So reads the bond. But if Texas suffers slavery to be extended over that part of her territory, then, when it becomes populous enough for admission, and is overspread with slavery, a new State may present a free constitution, be admitted by Congress, and before the slaves have time to escape, or to carry the question of freedom before the judicial tribunals, *Presto!* this free constitution will be changed into a slave constitution, under the alleged right of a State to decide upon its own domestic institutions, and thus the word of promise which was kept to the ear, will be broken to the hope. If Texas meant to abide by the resolutions of annexation, and to claim anything under them, it was her clear and imperative duty forthwith to pass a law, securing freedom to every inhabitant north of the compromise line. In this way only can the resolutions be executed in their true spirit. That territory is now in the condition of an egg. It is undergoing incubation. From it a State is hereafter to be hatched; but before promising to accept the chick, it would be agreeable to know whether a viper had impregnated the egg.

But there is a still further objection, of whose soundness I have no doubt; but should I be in error in regard to it, the mistake will not invalidate any other argument. The parties to that agreement stipulated on the ground of mutualitity, whout which all contracts are void .Some States were to be admitted to strengthen the hands of slavery, and some of freedom. A line of demarcation was drawn. Now, on investigation, I believe it will most conclusively appear that there is not an inch of Texan territory north of the stipulated line. It all belongs to New Mexico, as much as Nantucket or Berkshire belongs to Massachusetts. It was a mistake on the part of the contracting parties; if, on the part of Texas, it was not something worse than a mistake. The mutuality, then, fails. The contract is *nudum pactum*. Texas can give nothing for what she was to receive; and is, therefore, entitled to receive nothing but what she has got.

In regard to "the business of seeing that fugitives are delivered up," Mr. Webster says: "My friend at the head of the Judiciary Committee, [Mr. Butler of South Carolina,] has a bill on the subject now before the Senate, with some admendments to it, which I propose to support, with all its provisions, to the fullest extent."

Here is Mr. Butler's bill, with Mr. Mason's amendments:

A BILL

*To provide for the more effectual execution of the third clause of the second section of the fourth article of the Constitution of the United States.*

*Be it enacted by the Senate and House of Representatives of the United States of America in Congress assembled,* That when a person held to service or labor in any State or Territory of the United States, under the laws of such State or Territory, shall escape into any other of the said States or Territories, the person to whom such service or labor may be due, his or her agent, or attorney, is hereby empowered to seize or arrest such fugitive from service or labor, and take him or her before any judge of the circuit or district courts of the United States, or before any commissioner, or clerk of such courts, or marshal thereof, or any postmaster of the United States, or collector of the customs of the United States, residing or being within such State wherein such seizure or arrest shall be made, and upon proof to the satisfaction of said judge, commissioner, clerk, marshal, postmaster, or collector, as the case may be, either by oral testimony or affidavit taken before and certified by any person authorized to administer an oath under the laws of the United States, or of any State, that the person so seized or arrested under the laws of the State or Territory from which he or she fled, owe service or labor to the person claiming him or her, it shall be the duty of such judge, commissioner, clerk, marshal, postmaster, or collector, to give a certificate thereof to such claimant, his or her agent, or attorney, which certificate shall be a sufficient warrant for taking and removing such fugitive from service or labor, to the State or Territory from which he or she fled.

Sec. 2. *And be it further enacted,* That when a person held to service or labor, as mentioned in the first section of this act, shall escape from such service or labor, as therein mentioned, the person to whom such service or labor may be due, his or her agent, or attorney, may apply to any one of the officers of the United States named in said section, other than a marshal of the United States, for a warrant to seize and arrest such fugitive, and upon affidavit being made before such officer, (each of whom for the purposes of this act is hereby authorized to administer an oath or affirmation) by such claimant, his or her agent, that such person does, under the laws of the State or Territory from which he or she fled, owe service or labor to such claimant, it shall be, and is hereby made, the duty of such officer, to and before whom such application and affidavit is made, to issue his warrant to any marshal of any of the courts of the United States to seize and arrest such alleged fugitive and to bring him or her forthwith, or on a day to be named in such warrant, before the officer issuing such warrant, or either of the officers mentioned in said first section, except the marshal to whom the said warrant is directed, which said warrant or authority the said marshal is hereby authorized and directed in all things to obey.

Sec. 3. *And be it further enacted,* That upon affidavit made as aforesaid by the claimant of such fugitive, his agent or attorney, after such certificate has been issued, that he has reason to apprehend that such fugitive will be rescued by force from his or their possession, before he can be taken beyond the limits of the State in which the arrest is made, it shall be the duty of the officer making the arrest to retain such fugitive in his custody, and to remove him to the State whence he fled, and there to deliver him to said claimant, his agent or attorney. And to this end, the officer aforesaid is hereby authorized and required to employ so many persons as he may deem necessary to overcome such force, and to retain them in his service so long as circumstances may require. The said officer and his assistants, while so employed, to receive the same compensation, and to be allowed the same expenses as are now allowed by law for transportation of criminals, to be certified by the judge of the district within which the arrest is made, and paid out of the treasury of the United States: Provided, that before such charges are incurred, the claimant, his agent, or attorney, shall secure to said officer payment of the same, and in case no actual force be opposed, then they shall be paid by such claimant, his agent, or attorney.

Sec. 4. *And be it further enacted,* When a warrant shall have been issued by any of the officers under the second section of this act, and there shall be no marshal or deputy marshal within ten miles of the place where such warrant is issued, it shall be the duty of the officer issuing the same, at the request of the claimant, his agent, or attorney, to appoint some fit and discreet person, who shall be willing to act as marshal, for the purpose of executing said warrant, and such person so appointed shall, to the extent of executing said warrant and detaining and transporting the fugitive named therein, have all the power and authority, and be, with his assistants, entitled to the same compensation and expenses provided in this act in cases where the services are performed by the marshals of the courts.

Sec. 5. *And be it further enacted,* That any person who shall knowingly and willingly obstruct or hinder such claimant, his agent or attorney, or any person or persons assisting him, her, or them, in so serving or arresting such fugitive from service or labor, or shall rescue such fugitive from such claimant, his agent, or attorney, when so arrested, pursuant to the authority herein given or declared, or shall aid, abet, or assist such person so owing service or labor to escape from such claimant, his agent or attorney, or shall harbor or conceal such person, after notice that he or she was a fugitive from labor, as aforesaid, shall, for either of the said offences, forfeit and pay the sum of one thousand dollars, which penalty may be recovered by and for the benefit of such claimant, by action of debt in any court proper to try the same, saving, moreover, to the person claiming such labor or service, his right of action for, on account of, the said injuries, or either of them.

Sec. 6. *And be it further enacted,* That when said person is seized or arrested under, and by virtue of the said warrant, by such marshal, and is brought before either of the officers aforesaid, other than said marshal, it shall be the duty of such officer to proceed in the case of such person, in the same way as he is directed and authorized to do when such person is seized and arrested by the person claiming him, or by his or her agent, or attorney, and is brought before such officer under the provisions of the first section of this act.

AMENDMENTS *intended to be proposed by Mr. Mason to the bill* (S. 23), *to provide for the more effectual execution of the third clause of the second section of the fourth article of the Constitution of the United States:*

At the end of section 5, add:

And any person or persons offending against the provisions of this section, to be moreover deemed guilty of a misdemeanor, or in obstructing the due execution of the laws of the United States, and upon conviction thereof shall be fined in the sum of one thousand dollars, one half whereof shall be to the use of the informer; and shall also be imprisoned for the term of twelve months.

At the end of section 6, add:

And in no trial or hearing under this act shall the testimony of such fugitive be admitted in evidence.

It will be observed that the first section of the bill, after constituting the judges of the courts, the seventeen thousand postmasters, the collectors, &c., as tribunals, *without appeal*, for the delivery of any body, who is sworn by anybody, anywhere, to be a fugitive slave, refers to the before-mentioned officers in the words "residing or being within such State where such seizure or arrest is made." That is, the judge, postmaster, collector, &c., need not be an inhabitant of the State, or hold his office in the State, where the seizure is made; but it is sufficient if he is such officer any where within the United States. Mr. Butler or Mr. Mason, therefore, may send the postmaster of his own city or village, into Massachusetts, with an agent or attorney, who brings his affidavit from South Carolina or Virginia, in his pocket; the agent or attorney may arrest anybody, at any time, carry him before his accomplice, go through with the judicial forms, and hurry him to the South;—the officer, after his judicial functions are discharged, turning bailiff, protecting the prey and speeding the flight!

Still further; this bill derides the trial by jury, secured by the Constitution. A man may not lose a horse without a right to this trial; but he may his freedom. Mr. Webster spoke for the South and for slavery; not for the North and for freedom, when he abandoned this right. Such an abandonment, it would be impossible to believe of one who has earned such fame as Defender of the Constitution; it would be more reasonable to suppose the existence of some strange misapprehension, had not Mr. Webster, with that precision and strength which are so peculiarly his own, declared his determination to support this hideous bill, "with all its provisions to the fullest extent," when, at the same moment, another bill, of which he took no notice, was pending before the Senate, introduced by Mr. Seward of New York, securing the invaluable privilege of a jury trial.

I disdain to avail myself, in a sober argument, of the popnlar sensitiveness on this subject; and I acknowledge my obligations to the Constitution while it is suffered to last. But still I say, that the man who can read this bill without having his blood boil in his veins, has a power of refrigeration that would cool the tropics.

I cannot doubt that Mr. Webster will yet see the necessity of reconsidering his position, on this whole question.

Mr. Webster says: "It is my firm opinion, this day, that within the last twenty years as much money has been collected and paid to the abolition societies, abolition presses, and abolition lecturers, as would purchase the freedom of every slave, man, woman and child, in the State of Maryland, and send them all to Liberia."

The total number of slaves in Maryland, according to the last census, amounted to 89,405. At $250 apiece,—which is but about half the value commonly assigned to Southern slaves by Southern men,—this would be $22,373,750. Allowing $30 each for transportation to Liberia, without any provision for them after their arrival there, the whole sum would be $25,058,600,—in round numbers twenty-five millions of dollars!—more than a million and a quarter in each year, and about thirty-five hundred dollars per day. I had not supposed the abolitionists had such resources at their command.

I have dwelt thus long upon Mr. Webster's speech, because in connection with his two votes in favor of Mr. Foote's committee of compromise, which votes, had they been the other way, would have utterly defeated the committee, it is considered to have done more to jeopard the great cause of freedom in the territories, than any other event of this disastrous session. I have spoken of Mr. Webster by name, and I trust, in none but respectful terms. I might have introduced other names, or examined his positions, without mentioning him. I have taken what seemed to me the more manly course; and if these views should ever by chance fall under his eye, I believe he has magnanimity enough to respect me more for the frankness I have used. If I am wrong, I will not add to an error of judgment, the meanness of a clandestine attack. If I am right, no one can complain; for we must all bow before the majesty of Truth.

I have now noticed the principal events which have taken place in Congress, and which have led to what military men would call the "demoralization" of many of the rank and file of its members. Some recent movements have brought vividly to mind certain historical recollections in regard to the African slave trade, now execrated by all civilized nations. When the immortal Wilberforce exposed to public gaze the secrets of that horrid traffic, his biographer says, "The first burst of generous indignation promised nothing less than the instant abolition of the trade, but *mercantile* jealousy had taken the alarm, and the defenders of the West India system found themselves strengthened by the independent alliance of *commercial* men."—Life of Wilberforce, vol. I, p. 291.

Again; opposition to Wilberforce's motion "arose amongst the Guinea *merchants*"—"reinforced, however, before long by the great body of West India planters."—Ibid.

The Corporation of Liverpool spent, first and last, upwards of £10,000 in defence of a traffic which even the gravity and calmness of judicial decisions have since pronounced "infernal."

"Besides printing works in defence of the slave trade and remunerating their authors; paying the expenses of delegates to attend in London and watch Mr. Wilberforce's proceedings, they pensioned the widows of Norris and Gree, and voted plate to Mr. Penny, for their exertions in this cause." —Ibid. p. 345.

It is said that the Corporation of Liverpool, at this time, "believed firmly that the very existence of the city depended upon the continuance of the traffic." Look at Liverpool now, and reflect what greater rewards, even of a temporal nature, God reserves for men that abjure dishonesty and crime.

All collateral motives were brought to bear upon the subject, just as they are at the present time. The Guinea trade was defended "as a nursery for seamen."—Ib., p. 293.

Even as late as 1816, the same class of men, in the same country, opposed the abolition of "white slavery" in Algiers, from the same base motives of interest. It was thought that the danger of navigating the Mediterranean, caused by the Barbary Corsairs, was advantageous to British commerce; because it might deter the merchant ships of other nations from visiting it. After Lord Exmouth had compelled the Algerines to liberate their European slaves, he proceeded against Tunis and Tripoli. In giving an account of what he had done, he defends his conduct "upon general principles," but adds, "as applying to our own country, [Great Britain,] it may not be borne out, *the old mercantile interest being against it.*"—Osler's Life of Exmouth, p. 303.

So after Admiral Blake, in the time of Cromwell, had attacked Tunis, he says, in his despatch to Secretary Thurloe, "And now seeing it hath pleased God soe signally to justify us herein, I hope his highnes will not be offended at it, nor any who regard duly the honor of the nation, *although I expect to have the clamors of* INTERESTED MEN."—(Thurloe's State Papers, vol. II, p. 390.) And is Commerce, the daughter of Freedom, thus forever to lift her parricidal hand against the parent that bore her? Are rich men forever to use their "thirty pieces of silver," or their "ten thousand pounds sterling," or their hundreds of thousands of dollars, to reward the Judases for betraying their Saviour? Viewed by the light of our increased knowledge, and by our more elevated standard of duty, the extension of slavery into California or New Mexico, at the present time, or even the suffrance of it there, is a vastly greater crime than was the African slave trade

itself, in the last century; and I would rather meet the doom of posterity or of heaven, for being engaged in the traffic then, than for being accessary to its propagation now.

Let those who aid, abet, or connive at slavery extension now, as they read the damning sentence which history has awarded against the actors, abettors and connivers of the African trade, *but change the names*, and they will be reading of themselves. Should our new territories be hereafter filled with groaning bondmen, should they become an American Egypt, tyrannized over by ten thousand Pharaohs, it will be no defence for those who permitted it, to say, "We hoped, we supposed, we trusted, that slavery could not go there;" Nemesis, as she plies her scorpion lash, will reply, "*You might have made it certain.*"

On this great question of freedom or slavery, I have observed with grief, nay, with anguish, that we, at the North, break up into hostile parties, hurl criminations and recriminations to and fro, and expend that strength for the ruin of each other, which should be directed against the enemies of Liberty; while, at the South, whenever slavery is in jeopardy, all party lines are obliterated, dissensions are healed, enemies become friends, and all are found in a solid column, with an unbroken front. Are the children of darkness to be forever *so much* wiser than the children of light? In the recent choice of delegates for the Nashville Convention, I have not seen a single instance where Whig and Democrat have not been chosen as though they were Siamese twins, and must go together. But here it often happens, that as soon as one party is known to be in favor of one man, this act alone is deemed a sufficient reason why another party should oppose him. Why can we not combine for the sacred cause of freedom, as they combine for slavery? No thought or desire is further from my mind than that of interfering with any man's right of suffrage; but if (which is by no means impossible, nor perhaps improbable,) the fate of New Mexico should be decided by one vote, and my vote should have been the cause of a vacancy in any Congressional District that might have sent a friend to freedom, I should say, with Cain, "My punishment is greater than I can bear."

On the subject of the present alienation and discord between the North and the South, I wish to say that I have as strong a desire for reconciliation and amity as any one can have. There is no *pecuniary* sacrifice within the limits of the Constitution, which I would not willingly make for so desirable an object. Public revenues I would appropriate—private taxation I would endure—to relieve this otherwise thrice glorious Republic, from the calamity and the wrong of slavery. I would not only resist the devil, but if he will flee from me, I will build a bridge of gold to facilitate his escape. I mention this to prove that it is not the value, *in money*, of territorial freedom, for which I contend, but its value *in character*, *in justice*, *in human happiness*. While I utterly deny the claim set up by the South, yet I would gladly con-

sent that my southern fellow citizens should go to the territories and carry there every kind of property which I can carry. I would then give to the Southern States their full share of all the income ever to be derived from the sales of the public lands, or the leasing of the public mines; and whatever, after this deduction, was left in the public treasury, should be appropriated for the whole nation, as has been the practice heretofore. That is, in consideration of excluding slavery from the territories, I would give the South a double share, or even a three-fold share, of all the income that may ever be derived from them. Pecuniary surrenders I would gladly make for the sake of peace, but not for peace itself would I surrender Liberty.

It would be to suppose our merchants and manufacturers void of common foresight, could they believe that concession now will bring security hereafter. By yielding the moral question, they jeopard their pecuniary interests. Should the South succeed in their present attempt upon the territories, they will impatiently await the retirement of Gen. Taylor from the Executive Chair, to add the "State of Cuba," with its 500,000 slaves, its ignorance and its demoralization, to their roll of triumph. California will be a free trade State, by the most certain of all biases. They will have nothing to sell but gold; they will have everything to buy—from cradles to coffins, and all between. If New Mexico is slave, it will also be free trade; and Cuba as certainly as either—though in that island facilities for smuggling will reduce the difference between tariff and free trade to nothing. A surrender therefore, by our Northern business men, will be most disastrous to the very business that tempts them to surrender. Will they take no warning from the fact that their apathy in regard to Texas repealed the tariff of 1842? This is a low motive, I admit; but it may be set as a back-fire to the motive by which some of them appear to be influenced. There was no need, not a shadow of need, of perilling any principle, or any interest. Had the North stood firm, had they been true to the great principles they have so often and so solemnly proclaimed, the waves of Southern violence would have struck harmless at their feet. He is not learned in the weather who does not know that storms from the South, though violent, are short. We are assailed now because we have yielded before. The compromise of 1820 begat the nullification of 1832; the compromise of 1832 inspired the mad exploit of compassing Texas, which our greater madness made sane. The moral paralysis which failed to oppose the Mexican war, has given us the territories. If the territories are now surrendered, we shall have Cuba, and an indefinite career of conquest and of slavery will be opened on our Southwestern border. Every new concession transfers strength from our side to the side of our opponents; and if we cannot arrest our own course when we are just entering the rapids, how can we arrest it when we come near the verge of the cataract? The South may rule the Union, but they cannot divide it. Their whole Atlantic seaboard is open to attack, and powerless for defence;

and the Mississippi river may as easily be divided physically as politically into independent portions. With these advantages, let us never aggress upon their rights, but let us maintain our own.

Fellow-citizens, I would gladly relieve the darkness of this picture by some gleams of light. There are two hopes which, as yet, are not wholly extinguished in my mind. Beyond all question a compromise bill will be reported by the committee of thirteen, and will pass the Senate, and free California will be made to carry as great a burden of slavery as she can bear. It is still *possible* that the House will treat as it deserves this adulterous union. A single vote may turn the scale, and Massachusetts may give that vote. Not improbably, too, the fate of the bill may depend upon the earnestness and decision with which Northern constituencies make their sentiments known to their representatives, whether by petitions, by private letters, or by public resolutions. Let every lover of freedom do his best and his most.

Should the North fail, I have still one hope more. It is that New Mexico will do for herself what we shall have basely failed to do for her. If both these hopes fail, our country is doomed to run its unobstructed career of conquest, of despotism, and of infamy.

I have now, my fellow-citizens, given you my "Views and Opinions" on the present crisis in our public affairs. Had I regarded my own feelings I should have spoken less at length; but the subject has commanded me. I trust I have spoken respectfully towards those from whom I dissent, while speaking my own sentiments justly and truly. I have used no asperity, for all my emotions have been of grief and not of anger. My words have been cool as the telegraphic wires, while my feelings have been like the lightning that runs through them. The idea that Massachusetts should contribute, or consent, to the extension of Human Slavery! — is it not enough, not merely to arouse the living from their torpor, but the dead from their graves! Were I to help it, nay, did I not oppose it with all the powers and faculties which God has given me, I should see myriads of agonized faces glaring out upon me from the future, more terrible than Duncan's at Macbeth; and I would rather feel an assassin's poignard in my breast than forever hereafter to see the "the air-drawn dagger" of a guilty imagination. In Massachusetts, the great drama of the Revolution begun. Some of its heroes yet survive amongst us. At Lexington, at Concord, and on Bunker Hill, the grass still grows greener where the soil was fattened with the blood of our fathers. If, in the providence of God, we must be vanquished in this contest, let it be by force of the overmastering and inscrutable powers above us, and not by our own base desertion.

I am, gentlemen, your much honored, obliged and obedient servant,

HORACE MANN.

www.ingramcontent.com/pod-product-compliance
Lightning Source LLC
LaVergne TN
LVHW011132110826
845150LV00008B/2307

* 9 7 8 1 4 1 8 1 9 4 1 5 4 *